COUNTER TERRORISM

Terrorist Attack Response

Orlando "Andy" Wilson

CONTENTS

INTRODUCTION

It's a fact that terrorist attacks and incidents of terrorism are rising, and I expect that they will increase due to global instability and weak political leadership in many countries.

Twenty years ago, if we talked about terrorist attacks the chances are we would have been solely discussing IEDs, assassinations and attacks by recognized terrorist groups. But in recent years in addition to the threat from the official players in the terrorist world there is the threat from the lone wolves and the self-identifying terrorists. These individuals who have self-radicalized are in many cases off the radars of intelligence and law enforcement agencies. And if they are on these agencies' radars, they are classed as just being disturbed and in need of therapy.

With the help of social media, the recognized terrorist groups are able to groom their potential recruits globally with virtual anonymity. Social media also helps the self-radicalized individuals to motivate themselves, network and learn how to plan and execute their attacks. The terrorists will always have the advantage over front-line security personnel and law enforcement as the game of identifying the terrorists and the plans of their potential attacks is usually left to government intelligence services, who usually don't like to share too much of their data with others, for an array of reasons.

For the front-line security personnel, police and civilians who are lacking the intelligence insights on the identities and intended goals of known terrorists all they can do is rely on their personal security awareness, and ensure they have effective plans and procedures in place for dealing with suspicious incidents and actual terrorist attacks.

The boundaries of responsibilities must always be understood and respected when putting together any emergency plan of action. For example, when a terrorist incident is developing the overzealous civilian can hamper the police response or find themselves being mistaken for an actual terrorist.

Part of your threat assessment and response planning also needs to cover the issue of the professionalism, or lack of it, in the responding private security and law enforcement agencies. Remember, these responding agencies may have no experience or training on how to deal with a terrorist incident. Also remember, when things go "BANG" many well-presented boardroom experts and their fool proof plans tend to fall apart like a house of cards on a shaking table. So, you must understand that your personal security, that of your family and close associates is solely your responsibility.

Whether you're a concerned citizen, first responder or a law enforcement officer, you must compile a threat assessment for the environments in which you are living, working or traveling in. These threat assessments must be regularly updated. In time as you develop your threat assessments and plans putting them together will become more fluid, simplified and second nature, which is essential and your goal.

Most modern-day societies are seeking to demasculate their populations and make them dependent on the State for all their needs. This especially applies to people's personal security. In many places the police are actively dissuading the local population of doing anything to protect themselves and their families. If there is a problem just call the police, and hope they arrive in time to save you, right?

In many cases of active shooting incidents, armed civilians have shot and killed the terrorists and have saved countless lives. In many knife attacks civilians armed with improvised weapons have contain the attackers until armed police have arrived.

Your response plan to a terrorist attack needs to be flexible and you must consider the fight or flee options, and also the legal repercussions of all your actions. Remember, in places like the United Kingdom, the chances are if you severely hurt or kill a terrorist, while they are committing an attack you will be arrested, investigated and could face criminal charges if your actions were deemed excessive.

Your personal security, that of your family and close associates is your responsibility, no one else's! So, take the time to compile the relevant threat assessments for your home, workplace, shopping malls, means of transport, and locations you could be visiting etc. Then put in place simple and sensible response plans for if you are caught up in a terrorist incident or a direct attack. These days doing this should be common sense for all responsible adults!

Use this book as a guide to assist you in putting together your emergency plans. The contents of this book will make you aware of various terrorist threats and will give you simple and proven response options. Adapt your plans to fit your individual situation. All environments, situations and terrorist incidents are different, so your plans and responses need to be flexible as to be able to fluidly change as situations develop.

In addition to this book and others I have written on various personal security, close protection and law enforcement topics, I also supply an array of security training and consultancy services for private individuals, corporations and government agencies.

Orlando "Andy" Wilson

DEALING WITH BOMB
& IED INCIDENTS

My personal experience with dealing with terrorist bomb/improvised explosive devices (IEDs) incidents started in 1989 while serving in the British Army with 4 Platoon, B-Coy, 1-WFR for 22 months in Northern Ireland; since then bomb/IED awareness has always been a part of my security procedures and planning. I have to say that it astounds me these days after numerous, well publicized IED attacks globally that many security and law enforcement professionals are severely lacking in realistic IED awareness.

If you are working in the center of a large city, like London, Paris or New York, or are working in the emerging markets, where bomb scares are not unusual, it is likely that you may get caught up in a suspicious package or actual IED incident. Whether your venue, office or residence is targeted directly, or it just happens to be on the same street as a target for an IED attack, you will need to know how to react and should have procedures in place.

Improvised Explosive Devices are a threat to everyone and are used frequently and with great effect by criminals, cranks and terrorists the world over. If you follow international events, then you will see that there is a lethal bombing somewhere in the world almost every day. The basic IED can be made from commercially available materials that are sold over the counter in most places. Information on how to construct IEDs is available from military or survival bookstores, the Internet, former military, or demolitions trained personnel. The size of an IED can range from as small as a cigarette packet to as big as a large container truck.

IEDs can be disguised as virtually anything; this gives the bomber the advantage of being able to kill their targets without alerting them to the threat, giving the bomber a large degree of anonymity. IEDs can be used to kill selected targets or to kill indiscriminately. These facts are why the IED is often the favored weapon of criminals, cranks and terrorists the world over and is the most dangerous threat to security, law enforcement, military and the public.

In this book, I have listed some basic information on IED's and some basic guidelines for dealing with an IED incident. I also dissect the law enforcement response to the NYC Time Square car bomb incident in 2010. And after reading this chapter you should be a lot more knowledgeable and competent than those members of the NYPD who oversaw the response to that incident, well more of a circus than a response!

Explosives

There are many types of explosives available on the market, all of which have differing characteristics, chemical compositions and properties. What they all have in common is that they can be extremely dangerous. I am not going to go into the details of explosive composition because you don't need to know it; it makes no difference if a device has Composition B or gasoline in it, it's an explosive device and it can kill you.

There are two categories of explosives: high and low.

• High explosives such as Dynamite, Gelatin, TNT, RDX, PETN, C-4, and Semtex undergo a rapid chemical change upon detonation. This change is a transformation from a solid or liquid to a gaseous state. The change, which takes approximately one billionth of a second results in the gas rapidly moving away from the point of detonation at speeds of up to 26,500 feet per second, in the case of

C-4. The moving gas is the force that cuts steel, concrete and anything else in its path.

• Low explosives burn quickly instead of exploding. The best examples of low explosives are gunpowder and match heads. The burn rates of low explosives are usually under 3000 feet per second. Low explosives are usually more sensitive to heat, shock and friction than high explosives, which tend to be stable.

Commercial and military grade explosives are available on the black market either bought from corrupt soldiers/police or stolen. Also, you need to remember commercial explosives are used in construction, quarrying and by farmers and is available for sale from explosive distributors.

Bomb & Improvised Explosive Device Identification

Bombs and IED's can be disguised as virtually anything, so you need to identify whether you, your clients, home or office locations could be targeted for an IED attack. You need to compile a threat assessment and identify all the threats you could be targeted by, if IED's are in the threat assessment you need to start making procedures for dealing with an incident. You must remember when compiling the threat assessment to also think what other potential IED targets could be in your area, which if targeted could cause issues for you. I remember one client telling me that during the 90's in Colombia he booked into what he thought was a nice secure hotel only to look out of the window of his room to see it was next to a small military base, which at the time would be an ideal target for narco-guerillas.

At a personal level, you need to be aware and suspicious of any objects, cars, or activity in or around your locations that could be a cover for an IED. An unattended and out of place bag, an unknown car that has been parked next to your building or on an approach road too long, unknown people who are acting nervously etc. You must be aware and suspicious, but you must understand the realistic threats or, you will be seeing IED's and terrorists everywhere. Common sense is something which is lacking in people today in general but, as a security or law enforcement professional you need to be able to keep things real and not get caught up in what can be classed in many cases as group hysteria. So, at a basic level everyone needs to know what to do if they are caught up in a IED incident, how to deal with a suspicious object or in the worst-case scenario the aftermath of an IED attack!

Detecting IED's can be extremally difficult; there are many bits of equipment on the market that can sniff explosives, ex-ray bags and vehicles etc. These are all good if you have them, and if they are well serviced and maintained. As far as I know most of the "bomb sniffers" must be regularly calibrated and have their filters changed... I remember visiting quite a few high-profile locations in Abuja Nigeria, where the gate guards were using such devices to check cars, I doubt if the devices had been maintained since being taken out the box, and I would be surprised if they were even charged up. I paid numerus visits to a very high-profile hotel in Abuja and even though you had to walk through a metal detector it was clear if you looked at the power cable it was unplugged...

The best example of fake bomb detectors was the British Made ADE-651 that claimed to be able to detect explosives, guns, drugs, ivory and even truffles and was powered by the users' static electricity. You may laugh, but the Iraqi Government apparently bought £52 million worth of them. Its claimed that up to 20 different governments bought the fake device at £60,000.00 a piece... They were made by the British company ATSC, which was dissolved in 2013 and the company owner Jim McCormick was sentenced to 10 years in prison on fraud charges. So, if you use bomb detectors make sure they are real, are maintained and the people using them know what they are doing.

In my opinion the best thing for detecting IEDs and explosives are properly trained and handled sniffer dogs. Again, at a base level, the dog needs to be properly trained, looked after, and handled... I know of one company in UK that use to ask their guards to bring their pet German Sheppard's etc. on residential security details so the clients could see they had, what they believed to be professional dog handlers and trained dogs. I have seen Civil Defense sniffer dogs in Nigeria that were so afraid of the cars they were checking they had to be literally dragged to them. Always verify you're getting what you are paying for, of all industries the security and defense industry should be one of the most credible but, in many cases it's a scammers paradise.

The issue with using dogs and the man portable bomb detectors is you must get close to the potential device and within the blast range. This is a big issue if you are dealing with devices that could have been put in place just to draw security forces into an ambush or if you are dealing with suicide bombers.

The Secondary Device

Remember: The Secondary Attack, The Secondary Attack, The Secondary Attack!!!! If one incident has just occurred then expect another IED attack, a follow up ambush, an ambush on those responding or ambush on evacuation routes!

An IED can be used on its own or in conjunction with other IEDs or weapons. Good bombers will always place a second device near the first device, in a likely incident control point for security forces or on an evacuation route from the blast area of the first device. The second device is placed to ambush the personnel or emergency services coming to the aid of anyone hurt in the first blast, to target security forces dealing with the incident or personnel escaping from the first explosion. Sometimes the first device is placed and designed to go off for no other reason than to draw emergency or security services into an ambush or to drive people into a larger main device.

This happened in Northern Ireland with the Omagh bombing in 1998. Irish terrorists called in the location of a car bomb to the local police but with the wrong address, this resulted in civilians being evacuated from the suspected area of the IED into the blast area of the real device; 510 lbs of AMFO... 29 people were killed and over 220 injured... I have a good friend whose family lives in Homs Syria, where there have been too many car and suicide bombings to count. After one suicide bombing incident, the locals rushed to help the victims, one man came out of the blast area bleeding and screaming for help. When people started to pick him up to carry him to an ambulance, he blew himself up killing several of the civilians who went to help him, he was another suicide bomber.

I remember talking with a client/friend who had a relative working at a hospital in Orlando Florida on the night of the Pulse nightclub shooting on June 12th, 2016. After such incidents, the security for the casualty receiving hospitals etc. needs to be upped as they are a prime secondary terrorist target as are the responding ambulance crews. When republican Irish terrorists bombed Thiepval Barracks, Northern Ireland in 1996 they placed a secondary car bomb outside of the barracks medical center to try to maximize British Military casualties. Think about it, where will everybody be heading after a terrorist attack and if the terrorists murder the doctors and nurses who will treat the casualties? Terrorists do not operate by the same human rights they expect to be protected by!

You must always expect that if an explosive device has been found or has exploded that there could be a second or third device somewhere in the area, on evacuation routes or in incident control points etc.

Examples Of Incidents From Northern Ireland

Here are a few examples of how IEDs were employed by Irish terrorists; these are taken from when I was a teenager serving in the British Army in Northern Ireland between 1989 to 1991. There were many more incidents but at the time dealing with such things was the bread and butter work for the infantry battalions stationed in Northern Ireland.

• **9th of January 1990:** Olven Kilpatrick was murdered by terrorists in the shoe shop that he ran in the town of Castlederg, he was shot at close quarters. The terrorists left behind an explosive device in a shoebox set to detonate 30 minutes after the shooting, by which time security forces and emergency services were in the immediate area. Mr. Kilpatrick was an off-duty member of the Ulster Defense Regiment. Think about how many shoe boxes there are in a shoe shop! The device detonated and several Royal Ulster Constabulary (RUC) officers were injured, there were no further fatalities due to the fact that secondary devices were expected to be left at crime scenes and the area was evacuated.

• **15th January 1990:** A car bomb is detonated in the village of Sion Mills and causes major damage to the RUC station there, that was unmanned at the time. The responding security forces had limited routes they could use to get to the village. A QRF team from Strabane, led by at the time Cpl Lewis Weaver responded to the incident and on the way out spotted a suspicious white van along their route, it was noted, and they moved on at full speed. The same van was passed on the QRF's return route and the info was reported. On further inspection, the white van contained 1000 lbs of AMFO. It was reported several years later that one of the terrorists involved in the operation "Bernard Declan Casey" was working for British Special Branch and had ensured the command wire for detonating the device was not connected to the explosives in the white van… It was always expected for an IED to be placed along one of the routes into an area of an IED incident to ambush the security forces entering or leaving the area. If time was available, then routes would have needed to be searched and cleared. If time and helicopters were not available to deploy the responding troops, then the responding patrol had to drive in at top speed, if there were no foot patrols in the area who could get to the incident locations by moving across country.

• **1990:** A car is parked a short distance from the "Hump" security force base in Strabane with what appears to be mortar tubes inside. A security force cordon is placed around the car to secure the area and when the security force teams are conducting their 10-meter clearance searches around their cordon points, a team finds an IED attached to a trip wire. Further searches of the cordon positions turn up other IED's. The mortar tube in the car turned out to be a piece of drainpipe, it was a hoax that was used to draw security forces into the IED's that the terrorists placed in likely security force cordon positions.

• **4th May 1989:** Corporal Stephen Mcgonigle, a very respected member of 1 WFR, was killed near Silverbridge, South Armagh. A car was parked on the side of a country road in an area regularly patrolled by security forces. When the foot patrol spotted the car, they checked with their control room to see if the car was registered as stolen. It was not. The patrol saw nothing overtly suspicious with the car, so moved forward to check it out. At least one of the 4-man team was carrying electronic counter-measure equipment that can identify and block radio signals for remote-controlled bombs. This bomb was not remote controlled it was detonated with a command wire. The three other members of Cpl Mcgonigle's team were all injured in the blast.

You should take nothing at face value and always remember the secondary device. Always be suspicious of anything that looks out of place, if you are in an area where there is an active IED threat you need to draw up plans and procedures for how you will respond if you are caught up in an incident.

Types Of Device

Letter & Parcel Bombs

Up until the late 1990's the letter and parcel bomb were the most widely used of all IEDs. The bombers who use this type of device range from stalkers through to hard-core terrorists. The letter bomb gives the bomber a direct line of access to the target and affords the bomber virtual anonymity for themselves, as the device could be sent from anywhere in the world. As the name suggests, the device is placed into an envelope or parcel and posted to the target. Upon opening the device explodes.

Below is a list of things that should be checked for on any package that you suspect as being an IED. If you or your client is under a threat, all mail should be checked. If some of the following criteria are evident on a suspect package, it should be put through an x-ray machine to confirm or ally your suspicions. If you don't have an x-ray machine, then the suspect package should be placed in a safe area and specialist assistance sought. The package would have been knocked around whilst in the postal system, so it will be safe to move-just don't open it.

Letter and parcel bomb recognition check list:

- Were you expecting the letter or package?

- Was it delivered by hand, to avoid the postal system?

- Is it uneven or lopsided?

- Is the envelope rigid?

• Is there excessive securing material such as packing tape, string, etc.?

• Are there any visual distractions on the envelope such as company or official stamps?

• Are there any protruding wires or tin foil?

• Was there excessive postage paid?

• Was the address poorly written or typed?

• Any excessive weight?

• No return address?

• Any oil stains, discoloration or fingerprints?

• Any incorrect titles or any titles but no names?

• Any misspellings of common words?

• Any restrictive markings such as Confidential or Private?

• Any suspicious postmarks such as Belfast or Baghdad, etc.?

• Is the address stenciled?

• Any holes or pinpricks, which could be to let out explosive fumes?

• Any smell of almonds, marzipan or perfume used to mask the smell of explosive fumes?

• Any mechanical sounds?

Incendiary Devices

A simple form of this device can be made as small as a cigarette packet and be made from condoms and commercially available chemicals. When properly ignited, they will burn at high temperatures and are primarily designed to destroy property. Incendiaries require an initiator (flame or chemical action), delay mechanism, igniter and main incendiary charge. Incendiary bombs are usually used against shops and businesses for extortion purposes or say a lawyer's office to destroy case records before a trial etc. They can easily be placed between the cushions of furniture or among flammable objects, in the case of thermite it can be placed on or above machinery or vehicles, all devices can be timed to go off when the business is closed and empty of staff, so causing the maximum fire damage. This can also help to give the bomber anonymity as all the possible DNA evidence etc. could be burned!

If either your client or his business is under the threat of incendiary attack, the following precautions should be taken. A deterrent would be to install overt CCTV and employ high profile 24-hour security guards. The CCTV could, in the event of an incident, be used to identify the bomber but ensure to keep the recorders and data storage in a fireproof container or if using internet cameras back everything up on the cloud. If the client's workplace is an office suite, then access needs to be restricted as much as possible. Visitors should not be left unsupervised, all non-fire-retardant furniture removed, and all areas searched at the end of the business day. Cameras should be placed in high-risk areas such as entrances/exits and outside toilets and all personnel entering the office suite should be searched.

Blast Bombs

This device can be made very small. Blast bombs can easily be placed in a take away food container or bag and placed in a trash can or pile of rubbish, this type of device is used to cause disruption and confusion. In the city of London, UK, in the early 90s, a spate of such devices placed in trash cans resulted in all trash cans being removed from the streets and the London Underground. These devices can cause great disruption and kill indiscriminately.

Realistically, there is very little that can be done to stop a bomber planting these devices in city areas. The device can be easily disguised and moved during rush hour. It would be impossible to watch everyone, let alone search them, dogs could be employed but they will not be able to sniff everyone. Security cameras on buildings and in shops would be useful when trying to identify the bomber after the device has detonated.

Pipe Bombs/Grenade's

Pipe bombs are simply metal tubes filled with some type of explosives usually mixed with a type of shrapnel (nuts, bolts, nails etc.) and detonated by various means. If put together properly they can be very portable, concealable, and devastating weapons. Military grade hand grenades are available on the black market and are again very portable, and concealable with most having an effective blast radius of 10 to 15 meters. One incident that comes to mind is from when I was in Jos, Nigeria in 2011, where a church was attacked on Xmas Day... A grenade was thrown at a church and the police officer working security was shot and killed... A very simple terrorist attack that took seconds and where the attackers easily escaped.

You always must be aware of your environment and constantly assessing people around you and their body language. In high profile areas where the threat assessment has identified the possibility of this type of IED attack extra security measures need to be put in place such as screens on windows etc. so nothing can be thrown in and to minimalize the effects of a blast.

Undercar Booby-Traps (Uvb)

This device was a favorite weapon of Irish terrorist groups when targeting off duty police and military personnel. The device is placed in a container such as a Tupperware box and attached to the underside of a vehicle using magnets, usually under the driver seat. The usual method for triggering the device is by using a tilt or vibration sensitive switch. The UVB enables the terrorists to attack selective targets. There is a risk of discovery involved when placing this device as access to the targets vehicle is needed. If the bomber manages to plant the device, it will kill and maim the occupants of the car if it is not discovered.

The best defense against the UVB is to deny the bomber access to the vehicle. If you are under an IED threat and the vehicle is secured in a garage, the entrance and driveway to the garage need to be physically checked before the vehicle is moved. There could be a device attached to the door of the garage or a mine in the driveway. If the vehicle has to be left unattended, the surrounding area needs to be searched and then the vehicle. Searching a vehicle for IEDs is a basic and important skill and needs to be practiced regularly.

Car And Truck Bombs

Car and truck bombs enable the terrorist to conceal and move large devices. The car bomb can be used against individual or indiscriminate area targets. All it takes is for someone to drive the vehicle to the target and leave it to explode. Against an individual this device could be placed along a route or near an entrance to a building that is frequented by the target. The device can be triggered by remote control, command wire or, if the target is setting a pattern, by a timer. A method of delivering a device to a high security area is to use a suicide bomber or to force someone to drive the vehicle with the device in it to the target. The latter was a common tactic of Irish terrorists. It starts with the intended driver being kidnapped or having his home invaded. The driver is then informed that if they don't drive the device to the target location they and their family would be killed. If they drive the device, at least they hopefully have a chance of survival. The driver is then chained and locked into the vehicle with the device and is told how long they have got to get to the target before the device explodes. The driver has little choice but to drive the device to the target location and hope the security personnel there had at hand some bolt cutters etc. with which to cut them out of the vehicle before the device explodes. Nearly all front gate guard posts and check points in Northern Ireland in the day had bolt cutters available for exactly this situation. On 24th October 1990 our Battalions main base "Lisanelly Barracks" in Omagh was proxy bombed, the driver of the vehicle was cut out by the front gate guards. This 1500 lb AMFO device failed to fully detonate due to a faulty detonator.

As I stated earlier in major cities you can get caught up in IED incidents without directly being a target. You can just be in the wrong place at the wrong time. April 24th, 1994, I had just landed in Johannesburg, South Africa and was at the main bus station waiting for a bus to Durban. While I was talking to a girl I knew there on a payphone, I heard what I thought sounded like a bomb going off, and I was right, it was a bomb that killed 9 people just up the road from the bus station and I am sure injured way more. But the positive thing was, as I remember my bus still left on time.

While I was in Abuja and Jos, Nigeria in late 2011 and early 2012, there were numerous IED attacks on churches. There was one car bomb attack in Abuja that killed 37 people; the car had been parked in the church parking lot for days before the attack, but the area had never been checked or searched. A simple pre-service sweep by a trained search dog would have identified the device and prevented 37 people from being killed.

Improvised Mines

These devices can vary in size and be disguised as virtually anything. Their triggering methods are only limited to the imagination and ability of the bomber. In Northern Ireland, large devices were usually placed in rural areas in culverts, under roads, or disguised as milk churns or in bales of hay. In the conflicts in Iraq, Afghanistan and Syria IEDs have even been hidden in animal carcasses.

In urban areas, they can be placed in lampposts, rubbish bins or in vertical drainpipes on the side of a building. To place a bomb into a drainpipe, the terrorist lowers the device into the drainpipe from the top and a command wire detonates the device. The command wire can go over the building or be laid in the guttering connected to a firing point out of the line of sight of the killing zone. Command wires have the advantage over remote controls because there are no radio signals that can be identified or jammed, it's a direct wire to the device. In all such operations in Northern Ireland, the terrorists use youths as watchers. The child playing at the end of the street and shouting to his friends could actually have been telling a bomber that you were in their kill zone.

Sleeper Bombs

An IED can be placed in a position months before it explodes. If it is known that at a certain time in the future you or your client will be attending an event, a function or staying in a hotel at a certain time, precautions need to be taken. In 1984 in Brighton, England, such a device killed five people in an IRA attempt to kill the then British Prime Minister, Margaret Thatcher.

Defense Against Car Bombs & Mines

To beat the area car bomber, one must be vigilant and suspicious. If a vehicle looks suspicious, then get it checked out. Security forces have an advantage over private security personnel in being able to check out the background of a vehicle very quickly to see if its stolen or rented. So, if you are suspicious of a vehicle, call the authorities and let them check it out; if you are unwilling or unable to contact the authorities, then just avoid the vehicle.

For private security personnel: when the car bomb or mine threat is directed at your client, then precautions need to be taken. If there are limited routes in and out of the client's residence or office, then these routes need to be regularly physically checked. Any suspicious cars, recent digging or wires leading away from the road need to be checked out. When the client is traveling to and from work, the routes must be varied as much as possible. All trips should be kept secret until the last minute and then be preceded by an advanced security team, which needs to arrive at the clients destination with enough time to check out the area before the client arrives.

When entering or exiting a building, different entrances/exits need to be used. If possible, use fire escapes and staff entrances. If the client is to stay in a hotel, then their room will need to be searched along with the adjoining rooms if possible, and a check kept on anyone using the rooms. If the rooms are booked a while in advance, a check will need to be done on all building work and maintenance carried out in between the time of booking and the time of stay, as this work may have been used to cover the planting of a sleeper bomb.

Suicide Bombers

Suicide bombings are not a new issue, back in World War 2 the Japanese employed suicide attacks against allied forces to great effect in the Pacific campaigns, but in recent years suicide attacks have become the hallmark of Islamic extremist terrorists.

The Israeli security forces have been dealing with the threat of suicide bombings for decades and at a frontline level rely on training their police and military personnel extensively in reading and understanding peoples body language, to try to identify suicide bombers and eliminate them before they can detonate their devices. There is no politically correct way to deal with possible suicide bombers, luckily for the Israeli forces their Government understands their situation and supports their actions. This is a huge contrast to the witch hunts British Armed Forces have been subjected to over the last few years.

In the wars in Iraq, Syria, and Afghanistan the front-line troops had to constantly face the threat of suicide bombing attacks ranging from devices placed in armored vehicles to devices strapped to children. In such battles as the battle for Mosul the Iraqi forces had to deal with an extremely complexed situation as every vehicle and every civilian could have been a potential suicide bomber.

Kurdish forces in Iraq and Syria who were abiding by the rules of engagement advised to them by their Western NATO trainers put themselves at risk constantly by giving surrendering and wounded terrorist the benefit of the doubt rather than a quick double tap. The Kurds are seeking independence and were doing everything possible to fight a fair war against an enemy that deserved no quarter.

From a security professional's perspective if dealing with the threat of suicide attack's you must understand you are going to take casualties, but you need to plan to limit the extent of the casualties as much as you can. A good example of this is the attacks on the Coptic Churches in Egypt on Palm Sunday 2017, one surveillance video shows one of the bombers detonating his device at the security checkpoint. The bomber most likely realized he would not get into the Church without the device being discovered, so he decided to do as much damage as he could before arousing the suspicions of the security personnel.

So, at a basic frontline level everyone needs to understand what indicators they need to look for in someone's body language that could identify them as a potential threat. From a planning perspective, procedures need to be put in place to limit the bombers access to target areas and limit the potential blast area at checkpoints etc. in the case of an attack.

Mortars

These days no-one seems to consider the threat from mortar attacks. Mortars can be improvised, and I see no reason why terrorists should not be able to get hold of military mortars and ammunition. Mortars and grenade launchers have been found in the arsenals of Mexican drug cartels and recently in raids on illegal arms dealers in Spain, so they are available on the black market.

Improvised mortars were used widely in Northern Ireland, against Security Force bases and on mainland UK against Heathrow airport and the Prime Minister's residence in Downing Street, Central London. They were usually launched in quantities of ten, from an improvised base plate mounted on a flat bed or high-sided truck. These improvised mortars usually contained about 45 lbs of improvised explosives with a fuse time of 16 to 20 seconds and a flight time of 10 seconds. Their range was between 80 to 250 meters. The propellant was normally made from Sodium Chlorate soaked "J cloths". Each mortar weighed about 120 lbs and usually went straight through most anti-mortar screens.

Improvised mortar attacks were common in Northern Ireland, one of our patrol bases at the "Hump" in Strabane was hit in 1990 when D-Coy was on duty, Clady PVCP was hit when A-Coy was on duty, luckily no casualties on both occasions. The Irish terrorists tried the hit the "Hump" again in January 1991 when 6 Plt, B-Coy was on duty, the terrorist tried to put the mortars in a location where a RUC patrol happened to be having a tea break. After a quick exchange of fire where everyone missed, the terrorist escaped, but at least the attack was avoided.

Military mortars come in light, medium and heavy variations. I would say that light and medium mortars would be the most useful to terrorists as they are quite mobile. The maximum range of light mortars, 50mm to 60mm can be anywhere from 700 to 3500 meters when firing high explosive bombs of about 2 to 4lbs with rates of fire from 8 to 20 rounds a minute. The maximum range of medium mortars, 81mm and 82mm is up to 5900 meters with high explosive bombs weighing 6 to 8lbs with a rate of fire of 8 to 20 rounds per minute. The ideal targets for mortars would be busy airports, chemical plants, gas refineries and petroleum storage depots.

The best defense against improvised mortars is to identify and dominate any likely positions that could be used as a base plate location to launch a mortar attack, this can be done with CCTV, drones or patrols. If the terrorists have military mortars you are going to have a lot of problems controlling an area of up to nearly 6km around your location. This could be why no-one wants to consider the threat from mortars!

How To Deal With An Ied Incident

SECURITY FORCES SHOULD BE INFORMED AS SOON AS AN IED IS FOUND OR IF YOU HAVE GOOD REASON FOR SUSPECTING AN OBJECT OR VEHICLE OF BEING AN IED. DISPOSAL AND DIFFUSION OF IEDs IS TO BE LEFT TO TRAINED PROFESSIONALS. DO NOT ATTEMPT THIS YOURSELF.

Everyone should know the basic procedures for dealing with an IED incident. If you are working in or have a business in an area where there could possibly be and IED threat, you will need to draw up contingency plans for an IED incident. If you are traveling to a city where IED incidents occur, you need to know how things can develop and whether the local security forces know what they are doing or will be putting you and others at risk due to their incompetence.

There are four steps when dealing with an IED:

• **Confirmation:** Confirm, to the best of your ability, whether the object/vehicle is an IED, taking into account the following considerations: Are you under a threat from IEDs? Are the objects seemingly out of place? Are you in an area where terrorists are operational? Is there a funny smell around the object such as almonds, marzipan or petrol? This is where your threat assessment comes in. An unattended bag in an airport will arouse more suspicion then an unattended bag in a bar or restaurant but both could be just as dangerous or just as harmless. If all unattended bags in bars or other public places were reported as IEDs, there would be hundreds of false alarms every day but one just might be an IED. If you have good reason to suspect an object or vehicle, then check it out. The police and security forces should be willing to help you, if you give them good reasons for your suspicions.

• **Cordon:** Once a device has been confirmed, the area around it and roads leading to it need to be cordoned off so no-one can gain access to the area. It depends on the size and location of the device, as to how far away the cordon will be put in place, but a basic rule is that you should be out of line of sight of the device. This is because if you can see the device you can be hit by shrapnel or debris if it detonates. Think of the potential IED as a rifle barrel, if you can see it, it is pointed at you, and has a clear shot at you, so it can hit you. In the private security world, cordon preparations and duties would fall on the static or residential security teams etc. If an IED turns up at your residence, the residential security team would have to deal with the initial cordon and clearing of the area. Cordon equipment needs to be on hand, such as cordon tape, flashlights, maps of the area and communications equipment. Plans need to be made for the evacuation procedures and cordon points for the different types of device. All cordon and control point locations need to be physically searched for booby traps before being set up, the basic search would be 10 meters around the position.

• **Clearing the area:** People should be moved out of the blast area of the device; the blast area depends on the size and location of the device. In some cases, depending on the size of the device, it may be safer to leave people in buildings and under cover, rather than moving them into the open. It would make sense to assign a location in your building that could be used for this purpose, an internal room with no windows would be ideal. When evacuating people, a route should be taken that is out of line of sight of the device; if the device explodes when evacuating personnel, flying and falling glass is a big danger and needs to be considered when planning the evacuation route, as is the threat of secondary devices.

• **Controlling the incident:** Control of all IED incidents should be handed over to authorities, as soon as possible. You need to brief the responding police or security force personnel as to where the device is, when it arrived, how it arrived, where your cordon positions are, whether there is anyone still within the cordoned area and where they are. You also need to pass on any relevant information of threats that have been made and suspicious incidents or people that have been sighted in the area. Not only is this professional, but it could help apprehend the terrorists.

When a threat assessment reveals a threat from IEDs, a great deal of planning is needed. Whether you are a business owner, lone international traveler or a close protection team member, procedures need to be made for dealing with IEDs. Everyone in law enforcement, homeland security and the private security industry must have a basic knowledge of how IEDs work, the effects of an explosion and how to deal with incidents but, sadly they don't. These days basic search techniques and IED recognition is a necessity for everyone, as IEDs are the most widely used terrorist weapon and will be for a long time to come.

How Not To Do Things!

TIMES SQUARE CAR BOMB, NEW YORK CITY, MAY 1ST 2010

After reading what has already been written in this chapter you should be able to pick out quite a few mistakes in the New York Police Department (NYPD) handling of the 2010 car bomb incident in Times Square in the City of New York.

The vehicle that contained the explosives was a dark blue 1993 Nissan Pathfinder sport utility vehicle with dark tinted windows; it had been parked on a busy tourist-crowded street. People in the area noticed smoke drifting from vents near the back seat of the unoccupied vehicle, which was parked with its engine running and its hazard lights on. They also heard what sounded like firecrackers going off inside.

A police officer approached the car and observed the smoke, saw canisters inside, and could smell gunpowder. The vehicle was set ablaze, but the improvised explosive device had not detonated. Upon arrival, the bomb disposal team used a remote-controlled robotic device to break out a window of the vehicle and explore its contents. The device's ignition source had malfunctioned and failed to detonate the main explosives. Had it detonated NYPD officials said the bomb would have cut the car in half, and "would have caused casualties, a significant fireball and would have sprayed shrapnel, and killed or wounded many people".

OK, by 2010 the U.S. had been engaged in the war on terror for 9 years, so did the NYPD and other agencies not know how to deal properly with a car bomb incident. It amazed me when I saw the incident on the TV; they showed the bomb squad defusing the device with crowds stood watching. Basic rule, you and your cordon positions must be out of line of site of the device, if you can see the device you can be hit by shrapnel etc. If the device had detonated there would have been many un-necessary casualties because of the stupidly placed cordon positions alone.

The car bomb was described as a crude device, so was this the reason it was not taken seriously? My first thoughts if I came across a crude and amateur explosive device would be, where is the real one, and that the crude device was nothing but bait to draw security forces into a trap. I strongly doubt the area and cordon positions were checked for secondary devices. In the TV coverage you could see that the roads at either end of the road where the device was located were still open and cops were milling around and relaxing. A suicide bomber could have driven right through the cordon and blown up the bomb squad live on TV. You can't protect others if you can't even protect yourself! The NYPD's handling of this incident can be classed as negligent in the extreme and how you should definitely not deal with an IED incident!

If you are in an urban area and there is a car bomb incident you should initially find cover, get into a building and away from windows. If a device goes off the shock wave can break windows for a few blocks around it. You don't want to be on an open city street with glass falling on you from 50 stories up. When safe to evacuate the area use back alleys and non-obvious routes and do not hang around to watch how things develop. This is because of the threat from secondary devices and because the first device may only be there to draw in crowds of onlookers or channel people into the main device.

Conclusion

So, hopefully from this chapter you can see that dealing with IEDs is a complex problem where generally the terrorists have the advantage. The responsibility for IED and terrorist attack prevention is everyone's responsibility, not just that of the frontline security forces.

• Urban planners and the like are responsible for including basic security features in their designs be it for shopping malls or airports. Sadly, in places like South Florida security considerations seem to be the last thing on peoples minds; who's going to attack a beautifully designed airport anyway... Next you will be telling me terrorists will hijack planes and fly them into buildings...!

• Those responsible for security planning need to realistically understand the threats they could be facing and be allowed to put in place workable preventive measures and responses. I understand that a lot of times security management professionals have their recommendations for upgrading security procedures ignored by their senior management etc. But they must persevere, educate others and make maximum use of the resources they have at hand.

• Frontline security forces need the proper training, equipment, and workable procedures to do their jobs properly. Untrained and badly managed guards or police are not only putting themselves at risk but also those they are meant to be protecting.

• The general public needs to know the basics on how to identify suspicious activity, how to report suspicious activity and what to do if they are caught up in a terrorist attack. At a family level, there should be plans in place of what to do if there is a terrorist incident at a shopping mall or public gathering etc. Some simple knowledge and 5 minutes discussing plans and preparations can save lives.

Many thanks to former 1 WFR members Lewis Weaver (Moose) and Matt Trott for helping with details of the incidents from Northern Ireland.

ACTIVE SHOOTER RESPONSE

Remember!

Moving targets are harder to shoot than stationary targets!

Smaller targets are harder to shoot than a large target!

When I ask my tactical firearms students what the most important thing is that they must consider in a hostile incident, most reply that they should simply shoot the bad guys, get access to their weapons, shoot for the head, carry a big gun and so on. The answer I am looking for is that they should not get shot by the bad guys!

You should first of all work out a plan of action that you will take in the case of an active shooter or terrorist attack. Do this for your home, business and for when you are out and about in public. Things that need to be considered are means of communications, safe areas, when to fight, when to flee and so forth. Planning is what sorts the professionals from the amateurs, if you plan how to deal with a hostile situation, if it happens, you'll know what to do and how to react and should not be confused and panicked!

Plan A Reaction For Being Shot At!

As I just mentioned, you NEED to put together a plan of action on how you will react to a shooting or a hostile incident. Over the years I have spoken to many security contractors, police and former non-British infantry personnel and find it amazing that when talking about their reaction to fire drills most just say they would draw their weapon, if they have one and return fire...

That's ok if you have a gun or are on a gun range but you need to take a few other things into consideration if someone is shooting at you!

This is an adaptation of the British Army individual reaction to fire drill. Some of this may apply to you and some might not. Use this as a basic format. If you are serious about your personal security, you must put together a plan that is specifically designed for your personal situation and then practice it until it is second nature.

• **Preparation:** If you have a gun it must be clean, serviceable and well-oiled. Ammunition must be of good quality, clean and your magazines full. You must be properly trained and ready to deal with the incident.

• **Reacting to fire:** The immediate reaction at close quarters is to identify the threat, move to cover as you are deploying your weapon if you have one, and returning fire. If you are being shot at from a distance or do not know where the shots are coming from, you should:

- Dash: a moving target is harder to hit than a stationary target.

- Down: keep low and present a smaller target.

- Cover: Get into cover from fire.

- Locate: Observe where the threat is.

- Return fire: if you have a firearm.

• **Winning the firefight:** If you have a firearm: As soon as the threat has been firmly located, you must bring down sufficient accurate fire on the terrorist to incapacitate them or force them into cover so you can extract yourself from the situation.

• **Re-organizing:** As soon as you have incapacitated the terrorist or are in a safe area, you must reorganize yourself as quickly as possible in order to be ready for other possible threats. You need to reload your firearm if you have one, make sure that you or anyone with you is not injured and inform law enforcement and emergency services immediately.

Moving targets are harder to shoot than stationary targets. It's a fact, it's harder to shoot a target that is moving than one that is stationary. So, if someone is shooting at you, do not stand still, run, run, run. Smaller targets are harder to shoot than large targets! If there is no cover for you, make yourself a smaller target and drop to a kneeling position. I do not recommend prone position, as it takes too much time for most people to stand up. From a kneeling position, you can quickly run and get to cover.

There may be situations where you cannot evacuate the building you're in and you may have to find cover and wait the incident out. I have seen numerous gadgets being marketed that can be used to block a door in the case of an active shooter incident in a school etc. They seem to forget that most doors are made from light wood or alloy at best and will not stop bullets, if you look at the construction of most doors the average person should be able to punch through them with a bit of aggression. If you must barricade a door do it properly, so it will stop or slow down anyone trying to enter the room. I will talk about use of cover next, but you must try to hide or shelter behind walls or objects that can stop bullets, if you are in a drywall room, you might have problems. Try to alert people outside of your building to where you are, break windows if required, if you are on an upper floor and cannot jump to safety do your best to signal and alert the responding police and emergency services.

Use Of Cover

This is a very important and basic subject! In your home, business or when you are walking around, you should always be looking out for positions that you could use for cover in the event of a shooting incident. There are two types of cover: 1.) Cover from view. 2.) Cover from fire (bullets and shrapnel), you always want to locate the latter. You also may want to consider which type of rounds the cover will stop. A table might be able to stop a .32 bullet fired from a handgun, but a 7.62X39mm bullet fired from an AK-47 would go through both the table and you. Also consider will you want to be able to shoot through the cover, such as at a criminal in your house through dry wall etc.

Cover from view includes:

• Cardboard boxes and empty rubbish bins

• Bushes

• Thin walls and fences

• Thin tabletops

• Doors

• Shadows

Cover from fire (depending on the firearm used):

• Thick tabletops

• Heavy furniture

• Stone and concrete walls

• Dead ground

• Thick trees

• Various areas of a car

• Curb stones

One of the best-publicized examples of good use of cover happened in St. Petersburg, Russia on February 26, 1996. At 4:25 pm, two mafia gunmen in long coats entered a fashionable café. Under their coats, each man had a AKS-74. They were there to kill an opposing mafia boss, who was in the cafe with his two off duty police bodyguards. The mafia gunmen fired 60 rounds at close quarters from the AKS-74s and killed both the police bodyguards. The criminal boss tipped over a thick marble table he was sitting at and hid behind it; although wounded he was well enough to walk out the cafe making phone calls, after the gunmen had escaped. A Scottish lawyer was killed; he was just sitting drinking coffee in the café when he was hit by three stray bullets. The attack took about 40 seconds from the gunmen entering to leaving the café. The Scottish lawyer was just in the wrong place at the wrong time.

When you get into cover, you should always try to have an escape route and try not to get pinned down. When using cover as a shield, always keep low and fire or look around the cover and not over it. When you are in cover and need to move, first select the next piece of cover that you will move to and move fast and keep low. Keep the distances between cover positions short. When you get behind the cover, assess your situation, where the threat is, your next move etc. Keep moving this way until you are out of danger.

Remember!

• Always look for and make maximum use of available cover and concealment.

• Avoid firing or looking over cover; when possible, fire or look around it.

• Avoid silhouetting yourself against light-colored buildings, backgrounds and lights.

• Always carefully select a new piece of cover before leaving the cover you are in.

• Make sure you always have an escape route planned.

• Avoid setting patterns in your movement, for example, shooting or looking from the same position at the same level.

• Keep exposure time to a minimum; don't look over or around cover for an extended period of time.

• Always look up and behind you and remember that positions which provide cover at ground level may not provide cover from shooters in higher positions.

Camouflage

It makes me laugh when I see a lot of SWAT Teams and PSD guys wearing Tactical Black and other colors that look cool but do-nothing but make them stand out. In reality black is one of the worse colors to wear. What is black in nature? Look around you now and what in your surroundings are black? I expect very little... In urban areas most walls are white, gray or cream... Light colors! The colors you wear should blend in with your background whether its day or night. Even at night dark clothes stand out when moving past light backgrounds. In the countryside or bush, when moving through low bushes or open fields at night, the silhouettes of people in dark colors can be easily seen at a distance...

Moving Through A Building

If you have to evacuate your home or business, for whatever reason, it should be done quickly, quietly and with the minimum of fuss. You should also have already worked out your escape routes and exits. If there is an incident, get as much information as possible to what the threat is and where it is. I recommend you never use obvious evacuation routes and exits, the criminals or terrorists could have blocked, booby trapped, ambushed or manned them.

If you must walk down corridors keep low and move fast, do not walk down the center and do not walk next to the walls. Stay a couple of feet off the walls to avoid being hit by any ricochets and wall fragments if you come under fire. Doorways and frames can make good cover, even in an apparently empty corridor look for things that could be used as cover. Remember to continuously check behind you, and if you must stop, do not stand up, go to a kneeling position. Always be aware of where you are casting shadows, you do not want this to give away your position, such as before you go around a corner. You should always keep staggered spacing from anyone who is with you; you do not want to bunch up. Remember; one bullet can go through two people; large groups of people make an easier and more inviting target for the terrorists than a lone individual. Also, if you are dealing with criminals or terrorists who are using improvised pipe bombs or hand grenades, one of these devices could take out your whole group if you are bunched up and close together.

Going through doorways is very dangerous, especially if the room or area on the other side could contain a criminal or terrorist. If you must go through a doorway, try to determine if there are any threats on the other side before you enter. Use your senses of smell and hearing, in addition to sight; take a quick look into the room at a low level before entering. If you have to open a door, do so quickly, quietly and then back away from the door and listen. You want to back away from the door because if there is a terrorist in the room they will be shooting at the now opened door or moving if startled. Also consider if the wall around the outside of the door could stop a bullet; the criminal or terrorist could shoot through the wall and hit you, especially if they are armed with hunting or assault rifles. When you go through a doorway, again keep low and move fast, check the corners, when through the door move away from it and get behind cover.

You must keep a cool head as you might not be the only person evacuating the building. When you are clear of the building, get out of the area and summon support and law enforcement, ASAP.

Remember!

• Never use obvious escape routes.

• Use your senses of smell and hearing not just sight!

• Move quietly, cautiously and quickly.

• Corridors are areas of extreme danger to avoid whenever possible.

• If you need to use a corridor, NEVER walk down the center stay a couple of feet off the wall.

• If you must walk past an open door keep low and move fast.

• Always check around corners before you go around them and expose yourself.

• Continuously check behind you.

• If you must stop do not stand up, stay in a kneeling position.

• Avoid offering a silhouette for your opposition to shoot at.

• Lights behind you should be extinguished.

• Always keep a space between you and others; one bullet can go through several people.

Tactical Use Of Light

In my opinion, many people are over-enthusiastic in the use of flashlights. There is a big market in tactical flashlights and the companies making them wants everyone to buy one, thus making them a must have item. Flashlights have an application in hostile situations, but you should remember that any light will give away your position and draw fire. Light should be used sparingly and tactically. I tell my students to get used to training in the dark and using their senses of hearing and smell in addition to sight. At night there is more chance you will hear someone before you see them! When moving in a dark environment, do so slowly and cautiously and try to make minimum noise. Try finding your way around your house or business space in the dark, and before you start moving around give your eyes a few minutes to adjust to the dark.

If you must use a flashlight, keep it at arm's length and keep it on for no longer than necessary, then move quickly or get behind cover. If you want to check a room or a corridor, one option is to roll the flashlight across the doorway, the corridor or into the room. Light can be used as a distraction and help to cover your movement, shine it in the general direction of your opponent and move. This will mess up their night vision and if you leave the light pointing in their direction, it will be difficult for them to see what is happening behind the light.

If possible, use remote lights, this is more of an application for your home or business. For example, place powerful spotlights that illuminate corridors to safe rooms, stairways or doorways. If your home is broken into at night, you could move your family to your safe room and take up a position in cover behind the lights. If you hear or identify movement to your front, you turn on the spotlights; this will surprise, blind and illuminate anyone in the corridor. This will also help you to confirm that the people in your house are criminals, terrorists or the good guys and give you good targets to shoot at if you have a firearm in a hostile situation.

After A Shooting Incident

You should do all that you can to avoid getting involved in any hostile situations, even indirectly. If you are somewhere where a hostile situation is developing, leave the area quickly and not by an obvious route. You do not want to be in the wrong place at the wrong time and to catch a stray bullet. So, if you see a hostile incident developing and it has nothing to do with you, mind your own business and leave the area, ASAP!

The only exception to the above rule of avoiding hostile confrontations is if you are properly trained, armed, and by doing so, you will be protecting the lives of innocent people. It's a fact that armed civilians who have intervened in potential active shooter situations have saved the lives of countless innocent people.

If you are unfortunate enough to get involved in a shooting incident, when you believe the incident is over, you should reload your weapon if you have one, prepare to deal with any other threats, give first aid to anyone with you who is injured and evacuate to a safe location. You should also call for support and police etc. as soon as is safely possible.

Even if you believe others have already called the police, still do so yourself and identify yourself to the dispatcher as the victim of a hostile encounter and do as the dispatcher tells you, as long as it does not compromise your safety. You must ensure that the police officers responding to the incident know that you are the victim and not the attacker. For their own safety, the police officers will assume that anyone at the scene of the incident is a threat. You should never point your gun at the police and should comply with their every request. Remember the responding police will be scared and most are not that well trained and will shoot with minimum excuse. Try to remain calm and do not argue with them and do as you are told. Make no fast movements and keep your hands where they can be seen. It would be unfortunate to survive a lethal encounter with a criminal, only to end up being shot by the police.

If you get into a hostile shooting in a developing country where the police cannot be trusted and going to prison would most probably mean you would catch an incurable disease to say the least, you should have pre-planned on how to deal with the situation. My advice; leave the country as quickly as possible!

COUNTER-ATTACK CONSIDERATIONS

Fundamentals of the Tactical Assault

· **Fast and Fluid Movement:** Stay low and keep moving, fluid team movement comes from training, training and training!

· **Maximum Use of Cover:** Always use cover, always look up, always cover your rear, never stand in open ground and never stay in open ground… Get to cover!

· **Accuracy of Fire:** Fire accurate and controlled shots, don't waste ammo, don't spray and pray, every shot has a meaning and target!

· **Flexibility in Arcs of Fire:** You will sweep your people; trigger control is gun safety… Always be prepared for 360-degree contacts and defense! Sorry, but the bad guys don't read the conventional warfare rule books!

· **Accurate and Sustained Suppressing Fire:** Don't waste ammo, suppress the targets with accurate and controlled fire. Get comfortable working and moving with close fire support, closer the fucking better!!

· **Maximum Aggression on Target:** If it's a threat or potential threat kill it… If you need to capture a target have the necessary non-lethal weapons deployed and backed up with lethal weapons!

· **Rehearse, Rehearse, Rehearse……**

Basic Counter-Attack Considerations

There may be situations where if you are trained and armed when you will have to take aggressive action. For example, if involved in an ambush that disables your vehicles, to get out of the kill zone you may have to attack the ambush party. A terrorist attack on a residence where access has been gained by the attackers, the residents or security team must defend the building and possibly clear any attackers from within. A terrorist attack on a shopping mall or hotel where you may be visiting or staying where aggressive action may be required to evacuate the location.

This is very basic information and can help you establish your own procedures if you are in a situation where you have the capabilities for counter-attack options. This is based on basic procedures for close protection teams and can be adapted to most situations. You cannot learn the skills required for this by reading a book or this document, you have to learn to shoot and train tactically for these tasks. This section can help you establish your procedures; but you won't become a Tacticool Ninja by just reading this!

There are three fundamental elements to aggressive actions:

• Speed

• Surprise

• Aggression

For your action to be successful you must have at least two of the above elements.

Hostage Rescue Threat Assessment

1. Has the incident started?

a. If no:

i. What is the source of the information on potential incident, is it reliable?

ii. What actions to counter or intercept criminals will you take?

b. If yes:

i. What has happened?

ii. When did it start?

iii. Where is the location of the incident? Get maps, details etc.

iv. Who and how many criminals involved?

a. Ex-partner:

b. Work or college:

c. Friend:

d. Group:

e. Unknown:

2. Are the criminals armed?

3. For what reason have they taken hostages?

a. Publicity for a cause

b. Mental illness

c. Financial gain

d. Crime gone wrong

4. What demands have been made?

5. Have any other police or security agencies been informed and what action have they taken?

6. How as the incident progressed?

7. Possible type of action needed? Lethal or non-lethal, covert or overt

8.   What are limitations do you will have to work within?

9.   Manpower needed:

10.   Support needed:

11.   Time for rehearsals

Consideration For A Building Assault

Study Area – Map – Arial photos

Recce Drive By (Film)

1. Routes in

2. Approaches

3. Passby

4. Counter Surveillance location / CCTV

5. Routes out

6. RV

Foot CTR

1. Routes in

2. Drop off

3. Approach

4. Location

5. Counter Surveillance location / CCTV

6. Sniper/OP locations

7. Routes out

8. Pick up locations

9. RV

Assault

1. Team & Kit

2. Briefing

3. Rehearsals

4. Cordons & Cut-offs

5. Distractions

6. Route in

7. Drop off

8. Approach

9. Entry: Covert, loud or other

10. Clear

11. Re-org

Withdraw

1. Foot: Routes, CS, Pick up

2. Vehicle: Routes, CS, Switch

Post-Op

1. Defense

2. Debrief

3. Disperse

Mobile Counter-Attacks

The conventional military response to an ambush is to attack the ambush. In most cases an individual or small security team would not be able to attack an ambush, for to do so would leave a client or family members without close protection when the need is greatest. Also, an individual or two-man security team would not usually have sufficient weapons or ammunition to perform an assault.

The best means of attacking an ambush is to use a separate security team not responsible for the client's immediate protection. The counter-attack team should consist of people who have received training in small unit tactics and have sufficient firepower to deal with all threats. It should consist of no less than two people, in one vehicle. The counter-attack team follows the client's vehicle at a distance so that it will not become caught in an ambush on the client's vehicle but close enough to be able to attack the ambush quickly. The distances the team will have to be from the client will vary due to terrain, and traffic etc. The protective surveillance team/personnel can be trained and used as the counter-attack team.

Actions on a terrorist ambush by immediate close protection personnel:

• Return fire

• Drop smoke

• Cover Client's vehicle and attempt to break out of the kill zone.

• Send contact report

When counter-attack begins:

• Give covering fire.

• Remove Client from the killing zone to a safe location.

If the opportunity arises to escape before the counter-attack team acts, then do so. Never endanger the client because of your concerns for the counter-attack team.

Actions on a terrorist ambush by the counter-attack team:

• Move to the kill zone at best speed

• Use lights and siren for distractions

• Debus and attack the ambush party or drive at the ambush party location

• Do not hesitate. Fast, aggressive action is vital.

• If the client has been extracted, do not attack the ambush but give covering fire and escort the client to a safe house or emergency RV.

• Weapons. The maximum use must be made of automatic weapons, grenades and CS gas etc.

Counter-Attacks On Buildings

A counter-attack on a building must be mounted quickly; the longer the delay, the more time the attackers will have to fortify their positions. A counter-attack plan must be made and, if possible, practiced.

The counter-attack team should consist of at least two people, but not more than five; i.e. a team leader and two pairs. The team leader needs as much information as possible on the situation in the building. This could be obtained from civilians, the locations security team, or internal staff using radios or cell/mobile phones or social media posts.

The information required includes:

• The number of attackers.

• The description of the attackers.

• Method of entry

• Types of weapons and equipment used by the attackers

• Location of the client

• Physical state of the client

• Location of any family or household staff

• Overall casualties

Methods of Entry

• If restricted by residential security measures use same entry point as the attackers but only as a last resort.

• Enter by stealth whenever possible.

• Enter at the roof or top floor whenever possible.

• Immediate contingency planning to identify possible means of entry is essential.

• Secure the entry point.

Room Clearing

• Work in pairs.

• Clear the door.

• On entering the room clear the corners and move to cover.

• IDENTIFY all targets before engaging with fire.

• Check all hiding places.

• When room is clear, secure and lock the door if possible.

Progression

• Control will be difficult.

• Clear the building progressively, room by room, floor by floor.

• Stairs. Once taken, stairs must be held.

• Use fire and maneuver

• Avoid confrontation with other team members.

• Avoid being silhouetted or illuminated

• Use natural and the locations lights to your own advantage.

• Use sound to disorientate the attackers: 1) Alarms. 2) Sirens. 3) Concussion Grenades.

• Use of vehicles for approach and escape. 1) Must not spoil surprise. 2) Must remain secure. 3) Must not be put at unnecessary risk. 4) Consider for external lighting of the location

Action when building is clear

• Ensure that the Client is safe. Do not, however, remove them from a safe room.

• Check that all attackers are dead or secured as prisoners.

• Ensure that the perimeter of the building is secure. Secure the entry point(s).

• Decide whether to hold or escape

• Liaise and co-ordinate with external agencies on their arrival.

It is unlikely that plans proposed before the event will be put into effect as envisaged. Counter-attack plans must be carefully thought out and rehearsed by all members of the team.

SNIPER ATTACKS

I am sure there are those who initially looked at the title of this article and dismissed it as something that will never apply to them and that it is just fear mongering. Personally, I think the information here is applicable to everyone who is working in hostile environments or with high-risk clients. Examples of high-profile sniper shoots include:

• Zoran Đinđić, the sixth Prime Minister of the Republic of Serbia, was assassinated on March 12, 2003, in Belgrade, Serbia. Đinđić was shot from approximately 180 meters away, by a 7.62mm Heckler & Koch G3 rifle as he exited his vehicle outside the Serbian government headquarters. He was shot in the heart and died almost instantly, his bodyguard was also seriously wounded in the stomach by another shot.

• Kurdish crime boss Aslan Usoyan was killed in a sniper attack in central Moscow on January 16th, 2013. The assassin used a silenced 'Val' 9mm assault rifle. One of Usoyan's bodyguards reportedly returned fire with several blind shots, but the fact that it took some time for the police to find the shooter's position, showed that the bodyguard had failed completely at locating the sniper. Usoyan was shot in the head, a woman walking near the mob boss stepped into the assassin's firing line. According to LifeNews daily's timeline, the hitman attempted to move her by shooting her in the thigh. When she remained upright, she was shot again in the chest and fell, allowing the sniper to hit Usoyan once more as his bodyguards grouped around their wounded boss.

• Montenegrin gangster Dalibor Djuric was shot in the chest by a sniper on 22nd September 2016 while outdoors in the yard of the Spuz state prison in the Montenegrin capital Podgorica. The jailed

Mafia boss of one of the rival drugs clans from the resort of Kotor, was shot dead in prison while serving a two-year sentence for extortion. Police blocked the streets surrounding the Spuz prison to try to locate the assassin, but only found a car set on fire near the prison.

• Nicola Rizzuto was killed on November 10, 2010, he was the leader of the Sicilian faction of the Rizzuto crime family in Montreal, Quebec, Canada. Rizzuto was killed at his home when a single bullet from a sniper's rifle, that went through two layers of glass in the rear patio doors of his house before hitting him. The gunman had been hiding in the woods outside the mafia boss's Montreal house.

Three of the above assassinations were of Mafia bosses, and I am sure there are plenty of you wondering why I would use these as examples for legitimate close protection personnel. Well, 1. To show that the criminals have trained shooters and weapons available. 2. A lot of businesses overlap into the criminal world ranging from high-end jewelers to real estate agents. This is where you need to always do in-depth due-diligence on your clients, they may appear to be squeaky clean but, what's the real reason they need your services? So, understanding a little about snipers and counter sniper operations is an essential part of your operational planning and preparations.

Snipers

One thing I find amusing and annoying, is that whenever there is a terrorist attack with the attacker using a long gun, the media tends to immediately label the shooter as a sniper. There is a very big difference between a trained sniper and some idiot with a rifle! Also, just because someone served in the military to some extent, it does not make them a sniper. But, with modern weapons and a little knowledge, the wannabe jihadist or anarchist are still a serious threat.

Whether your potential threat is from specially trained personnel outfitted with state of the art equipment, or an individual with average marksmanship skills, armed with an off the shelf rifle, with tactics acquired from YouTube, you need to have plans in place to minimalize the threat, and procedures in place for dealing with active shooter situations.

There are five general types of shooters: the military sniper, the trained infantryman, the trained marksman, the trained shooter and the untrained armed civilian. Tactically each group have their own application and operational styles, you need to understand a little how they operate to identify the threat you could be under and plan effective countermeasures.

• **Military Snipers:** At the top of the sniper field are those who have been selected for and passed military sniper schools that usually last anywhere from two to three months. Note, I said selected for... Candidates for most military sniper schools are usually selected to attend the courses after going through basic training and proving themselves capable soldiers within their units, to start with. In addition to long range shooting skills military trained snipers need to be experts in navigation, communications, camouflage, concealment and observation. These individuals are trained to select key individuals as their targets, stalk them and kill them at distance while avoiding detection.

• **The Trained Infantryman:** Infantry soldiers from professional armies should have no problems shooting and hitting a man-sized target at 300 meters (yards) with their service weapons in most weather conditions from a prone position. In addition to their shooting skills they are trained in camouflage, concealment, stalking and combat tactics.

• **The Trained Marksman:** Most law enforcement units and the like tend to have marksmen as part of their tactical units that should be trained in precision shooting past 300 meters. The law enforcement sniper schools last from 5 to 10 days and are commercially available to those who qualify. These schools put an emphasis on precision shooting at 100 to 300 meters, and do not put an emphasis on camouflage, concealment, stalking and combat tactics which are not needed by law enforcement units.

• **The Trained Shooter:** Most military personnel are trained to safely use, shoot, and qualify with a rifle on a regular basis, so they are trained to some extent, but the standards can vary to extremes. There are also the trained competition and recreational shooters who practice regularly and undertake professional marksmanship training but lack the tactical training. Hunters also fall into this category and tend to have at least a basic knowledge of camouflage and concealment.

• **The Armed Civilian:** These are shooters with little or no formal military or firearms training. You can see them all the time in the news reports from various international war-zones. They have been given a rifle and ammunition and told which direction to shoot and that's about it. Their shooting is not accurate, they seldom deliberately target specific individuals, but they have high potential to cause casualties far out of proportion to their actual skill level at close and medium ranges.

Hopefully you can see from the descriptions above there is a lot more to being a sniper than just being able to hit a target at 100 meters, and having your picture taken wearing a Walmart ghillie suit. What makes snipers extremely dangerous is their ability to be undetectable before and after killing their target. If you don't know where the threat is, how can you counter it?

The art of field-craft is the bread and butter of the sniper's business. They can move undetected and have the discipline to stay virtually motionless and alert for hours, if not days at a time, to get a shot, this is what sets the professional sniper apart from the trained marksman.

The Tools Of The Trade

The typical range for a military sniper attack is 300 to 600 meters with medium-caliber rifles. But depending on the environment, the weapons available, and the skill of the sniper, undetected shots from 50 to 2500 meters plus are all possible.

Some of the main calibers for sniper rifles are:

•.22: Even though this is a very small caliber .22 rifles make excellent close range sniper rifles, as they are small and easy to suppress. Within 100 meters with quality ammunition, they should be able to deliver lethal head shots.

•.308/7.62x51mm: This round has been around since the 1950's and for many years was the standard round for NATO sniper rifles. This round, with the right weapon and shooter, can hit individuals at 800 meters and deliver harassing fire at 1000 meters plus.

• 7.62X54mm: The Russian military first introduced the 7.62X54mm round in 1891 and it is still in use today with the Dragunov sniper rifle and the PKM machine gun. When fired from quality sniper rifles the round is accurate out to 800 meters plus, I say quality because there are many inferior copies of the Dragunov on the market.

•.338 Lapua: The .338 Lapua has gained popularity as a sniper rifle cartridge and has been used extensively in the wars in Iraq and Afghanistan. In November 2009, in Helmand Province, Afghanistan, a British Army sniper, Corporal Craig Harrison, killed two Taliban machine gunners at a range of 2,475 meters using a L115A3 Long Range Rifle. This is the current record for the longest recorded sniper kill. The .338 round fired from military sniper rifles should be consistently accurate at ranges of 1500 meters but as you can see from Corporal Harrison shooting, it can reach out farther in skilled hands and in the right conditions.

• **9X39mm:** This is a Russian round that is used in the suppressed VSK-94 & VSS Vintorez rifles which have an effective range of 400 meters and has been in use by Russians and others since 1987. The 9X39 is a heavy, subsonic round that has excellent penetration qualities against body armor.

• **14.5mm:** The 14.5×114mm was developed in Russia during the cold war for heavy machine guns and anti-material rifles and is still used by many countries. There are numerous rifles chambered in this round with the average effective range of about 2000 meters against vehicles etc.

•**.50 Browning:** The .50 Browning round was first developed as a heavy machine gun round in 1918 and today it's still in service internationally. In the Vietnam war USMC sniper Carlos Hathcock used a scoped M2 Browning machine gun to get a confirmed kill at 2250 meters. In the 1980's Barrett developed the M82 sniper rifle that has been used extensively in conflicts since then. These days they are quite a few manufacturers producing .50 sniper rifles for military, police, and commercial use. Sadly, many of these weapons have found their way into the hands of international terrorists. The average effective range of a quality .50 sniper rifle is about 1800 meters.

• **20mm:** There are several rifles on the market chambered in 20mm, the American made Anzio has a reported maximum effective range of 5000 meters. There are several bullpup 20mm rifles such as the South African Denel NTW-20 and the Croatian RT-20 which would be a more maneuverable option for sniper operations but at approximately 19 kg (42 lbs) without ammunition they are not really stalking weapons. These weapons are meant for targeting vehicles, equipment and buildings. Vehicle mounted or in fixed positions, these rifles could be used with devastating effect, as their ability to shoot through most common building materials would render ineffective most cover from fire positions.

There is a lot more to distance shooting that just having a scoped rifle and ammunition, you must ensure the rifle shoots straight to start with. I was chatting with a friend who had spent time in Syria with the Kurdish YPG and he mentioned how a lot of the sniper rifles the Kurds had were not accurate, which is common in such settings. I expect a lot of the weapons were old and had been banged around which is detrimental to a scoped rifle.

Scoped rifles need to be zeroed regularly to ensure the rounds are going where you want them. If the optics are damaged or not properly fitted this can also lead to inaccuracy. The rifle's barrel needs to be in good condition and taken care of; Romanian rifles used to have very low-quality steel in their barrels, which lead to accuracy issues after minimal use. Ammunition needs to be of good quality, in many conflicts ammunition will come from various sources including the black market. Different ammunition will perform differently from the same rifle and old or damaged ammunition just might not be able to fly straight at all.

The weapon's sights are extremely important, and the weapon needs to be zeroed to the shooter. If the shooters eyes are good with quality open sights, they should be able to hit a man-sized target at ranges of 200 to 300 meters. For precision and long-distance shooting optics are a necessity and on the commercial market there are a vast array of scopes to fit all budgets. The quality of night sights have drastically improved over the last 20 years and they have become freely available on the commercial market. Simple and low-cost optics will not enhance the performance of the average $500.00 rifle into the accuracy class of a true precision sniper weapon, but these sights make the trained marksman a much more effective shooter at combat ranges out to 300 meters and beyond.

Many military sniper rifles are equipped with effective suppressors to either completely silence or greatly reduce the noise and muzzle blast of the weapon. Weapons such as the Russian VSK-94 & VSS Vintorez rifles have integrated suppressors on their barrels. Not only do suppressors reduce the noise of a weapon being fired, they also inhibit the task of trying to determine the location of a sniper. Suppressors can reduce the maximum effective range of a sniper rifle, but can be very effective when employed at less than 300 meters. Suppressors are available on the civilian market and are easy to manufacture, the legalities of ownership vary from location to location.

Countering Snipers

The first step in countering snipers is for everyone to be aware of the threat. This is where a threat assessment needs to be compiled and the realistic threats need to be identified, if potential snipers are a threat, then procedures need to be put in place. In general, operational planning for a sniper threat should always be considered to some extent. Not only should counter sniper procedures be planned for but they need to be practiced, your people need to be trained at least in the basic reactions to fire and the use of cover, preferably before they are exposed to the sniper threat.

When compiling your threat assessment check media reports and talk with locals and those with knowledge of your area of operations. You need to determine what the threat level could be; are there trained personnel, what weapons are available and what's their motivation and objectives.

When planning counter sniper operations, you need to answer four basic questions that will help you to assemble effective procedures that are relevant to your situation.

• What is your task and objective?

• What equipment and weapons do you have?

• What does your opposition want to accomplish and what capabilities do they have?

• What are the rules of engagement?

Rules of engagement are a very important consideration and can vary greatly, for example if you are caught up in an active sniper situation in an urban area in the US and you have a legal weapon on you, you cannot go blindly firing into potential sniper locations without positively identifying your target. Also, this puts you at risk of being mistaken for the active shooter and shot by police or other armed citizens. In a hostile or combat environment, your rules of engagement could be a lot freer but the limits of appropriate use of force need to be understood by everyone.

In many parts of the world people openly carry firearms and just because someone has a firearm it does not make them a threat. Also, just because someone is shooting, it does not mean they are shooting at you or being hostile. There is a big difference between someone in your vicinity shooting in the air and you being shot at with accurate and effective fire. You need to be able to determine the difference and plan your reactions accordingly.

Counter sniper procedures are mainly common sense and should be ingrained in most former military personnel with any hostile environment experience. Basically, if you can't be seen, you can't be shot, so limit your exposure, always make maximum use of cover, and move tactically. Remember, the sniper always has the initiative unless detected and is trained to wait for hours for a target or the time when your guard is down.

• Use concealed routes

• Avoid open plazas and intersections

• Stay away from, and don't linger in doorways and windows

• Move along the side of streets, not down the center

• Stay in the shadows.

• When moving with others stay spread out and use bounding over watch

• Go around well-lit areas at night

• Never be silhouetted against lights, skyline or light backgrounds

• Move quickly and quietly across open areas that cannot be avoided

• Make maximum use of cover and concealment

• Do not gather with others in large groups in the open

• Conduct all meetings, and gatherings of personnel undercover

• Do not wear anything that could draw attention to you

• Do not establish routines

After your threat assessment has been compiled you need to survey the area around your location for potential firing positions that a threat sniper could use, with routes in and out of those locations. Once identified, those locations need to be monitored and where possible, occupied with friendly forces, booby trapped or made unusable for a threat sniper. Clear any bushes or obstructions etc. that could be used as cover by snipers or inhibit your view of potential sniper positions.

Now in many urban and rural locations the potential positions for threat snipers will be endless, so your only option will be to limit exposure; if you can't be seen you can't be shot! Board up windows or put up screens to block the lines of sight for threat snipers. Canvas or plastic sheets can be used to make a dangerous alleyway or street crossing safer. In the long term, fixed positions, more solid barriers and defenses can be put in place such as sandbags, or earth filled 55-gallon drums etc.

Here are some basic military considerations for counter sniper procedures that can be adapted to the civilian world. As always, not everything will apply to everyone and all situations.

• **Cameras:** These days' surveillance cameras are widely available and can be used to monitor potential sniper positions. Hunters trail cameras can be placed in potential sniper positions and along the routes to those positions to help identify any potentially hostile activity in your area. Also, after a shooting incident they will help identify the shooter. In hostile environments, special care needs to be taken when checking or retrieving cameras as they could have been booby trapped, or the sniper could be waiting for you. Placing semi-camouflaged cameras around a property will let any potential threats know the area is monitored and can be a deterrent.

• **Drones:** Where weather conditions and budget allow, drones fitted with surveillance or preferably thermal imaging cameras are ideal for spotting potential threats especially in rural areas.

• **Observation:** Potential sniper firing positions should be constantly under surveillance and where manpower allows observers should be employed to monitor these positions for suspicious activity.

• **Patrols:** Random patrols should be employed to gather intelligence, identify hostile movements in your area and deny snipers access to firing positions.

• **Dogs:** Trained dogs can quickly search large areas and buildings for snipers who are trying to remain undetected.

• **Protective Clothing:** Ballistic vests and helmets will not always stop a sniper bullet, especially from large caliber weapons, but can significantly reduce the severity of wounds.

• **Armored Vehicles:** Whenever possible try to use armored vehicles.

Reaction To Fire

Over the years, I have spoken to many security contractors, police and military personnel and find it amazing that when talking about their reaction to fire drills most of them just say they would draw their weapon and return fire etc. That's ok on a gun range, but you need to take a few other things into consideration if someone is shooting at you! You also need to remember that if you are being targeted by a competent marksman unless you have detected them before they pull the trigger, the chances are you're going to be dead or seriously injured.

The basics, moving targets are harder to shoot than stationary targets. It's a fact, it's harder to shoot a target that is moving than one that is stationary. So, if someone is shooting at you, do not stand still, run, and get into cover. Smaller targets are harder to shoot than large targets! If there is no cover for you, make yourself a smaller target and drop to a kneeling or prone position.

The following is an adaptation of the British Army individual re-action to fire drill. Some of this may apply to you and some might not- use this as a basic format. If you are serious about your personal security, you must put together a plan that is specifically designed for your situation and then practice it until it is second nature.

• **Preparation:** If you have a gun, it must be clean, serviceable and well-oiled. Ammunition must be of good quality, clean and your magazines full. You must be properly trained and ready to deal with the incident.

• **Reacting to fire:** The immediate reaction at close quarters is to identify the threat, move to cover as you are deploying your weapon if you have one, and returning fire. If you are being shot at from a distance or do not know where the shots are coming from, you should:

- Dash- A moving target is harder to hit than a stationary target.

- Down- Keep low and present a smaller target.

- Cover- Get into cover from fire.

- Locate- Observe where the threat is.

- Return fire- If you have a firearm.

• **Winning the firefight:** If you have a firearm: As soon as the threat has been firmly located, you must bring down sufficient accurate fire on the terrorist to incapacitate them or force them into cover so you can extract yourself from the situation.

• **Re-organizing:** As soon as you have incapacitated the terrorist or are in a safe area, you must reorganize yourself as quickly as possible in order to be ready for other possible threats. You need to reload your firearm if you have one, make sure that you or anyone with you is not injured and inform, support personnel, law enforcement and emergency services immediately.

Where the rules of engagement allow, suppressing fire can be directed at the general area of the sniper's location to force them into or keep them behind cover, so you can move to a safer cover position, or extract from the sniper's kill zone. Look for and shoot at objects close to the sniper's position that would cause ricochets and flying debris, such as brick, plastered or concrete walls. Also, you need to be aware of injuries from ricochets and debris when being shot at! In hostile environments and combat zones maximum use should be made of what light, medium and heavy weapons are available.

Make maximum use of smoke dischargers where available and use the smoke to cover your movement. Commercial smoke signals are available from maritime stores as they are used for emergency signals on boats, also various smoke bombs are used for paintball and airsoft games. In a major city the chances are you cannot carry firearms, but you can legally carry a couple of smoke bombs. If an active shooter situation develops drop smoke and bugout!

It is very important that you understand the difference between cover from view and cover from fire; you always want to locate the latter where possible. You need to consider which type of rounds will be stopped by the cover you're using. A table might be able to stop a .32 fired from a handgun, but a .50 round from a M82 will go through it and you.

If planning the defense for a building, you need to consider what caliber of rounds the inner and outer walls can stop. Also, where large caliber rounds can penetrate walls, you can expect bricks and plaster to splinter within the rooms and cause injuries. You also need to take note of any surfaces that would cause incoming rounds to ricochet within the building.

Cover from view means you can't be seen but can be shot and includes:

• Cardboard boxes and empty rubbish bins

• Bushes

• Thin walls and fences

• Thin tabletops

• Doors

• Shadows

Cover from fire means, depending on the firearm used, you can't be seen or shot and includes:

• Thick tabletops

• Heavy furniture

• Stone and concrete walls

• Dead ground

• Thick trees

• Various areas of a car

• Curb stones

• Re-enforced barriers

When you get into cover, you should always try to have an escape route and try not to get pinned down. When using cover as a shield, always keep low and fire or look around cover- not over it. When you are in cover and need to move, first select the next piece of cover that you will move to and move fast and keep low. Keep the distances between cover positions short. When you get behind the cover, assess your situation, where the threat is, etc. Keep moving this way until you are out of danger.

Hunting The Hunters

When a sniper threat has been identified and you have the trained personnel, weapons and are within your rules of engagement, you should take active measures to eliminate or capture the sniper. Potential indicators that threat snipers are in your area could be:

• Personnel seen wearing camouflage uniforms

• Individuals in possession of binoculars, range-finders, and well-maintained scoped rifles

• Hearing single-shots being fire.

• A lack of locals in an area before a shooting incident

• Reflections spotted from optical lenses

• Small groups of (one to three) local personnel wandering around or observing your location for no apparent reason.

To capture or eliminate a threat sniper you need to identify a pattern in their modus operandi such as:

• Time of day of sightings or shooting

• Direction of incoming sniper fire

• Location of threat sniper sightings

• Patrols would need to look for material evidence of threat snipers being in a location such as broken foliage, hide positions, cigarette butts, food, body waste, empty round casings or discarded equipment

Once a pattern in the sniper's routine has been identified, be it the location of a potential firing position, a route in or out of that position, then a covert ambush would need to be set, and the sniper killed or captured. Note: Kill or capture operations need to be kept on a need-to-know basis, regular routines need to be maintained as not to alert the threat sniper or surveillance that they are being targeted.

Conclusion

Hopefully this article has given you an insight into counter-sniper operations and will enable you to draw up some plans and procedures to fit your needs and circumstances. Sadly, we all need to keep the threat from active sniper shooting in mind and be prepared to deal with worse case scenarios.

STABBING ATTACKS

Terrorists and criminals will always find weapons to commit their atrocities, be it guns, knives, cars, chemicals or rocks. Mass knife attacks and knife crime in general has risen greatly over the last few years, especially in Western Europe, mainly due to open immigration policies, diluted policing and lenient criminal court systems.

Once upon a time stabbings in countries like the United Kingdom were extremely rare, but now stabbings are a daily occurrence in most major cities. Youth gangs and immigrants blatantly promote the knife crime culture. When I was growing up in rural UK almost everyone carried a pocketknife, we used to take them to school. Were there fights at school? Of course, boys fight. Did anyone ever get stabbed? Never!

The government response to knife crime in places like the United Kingdom is to criminalize knives as it's far easier than dealing with the social problems behind the knife gang culture, radicalized individuals and groomed terrorists. Governments tend to always blame everyone else for their countries problems and look for a quick fix, instead of looking and addressing the real issues. In the case of the United Kingdom the real issues include poor parenting, a lack of moral values within the society, an undisciplined educational system, weak policing and enforcement of laws, and a court system that is working for a woke government agenda rather than for the good of the majority of law-abiding people.

In a society where firearms can be legally carried for self-defense, the response to a knife attack is to clearly identify and shoot the attacker. But, in unarmed societies things are not so simple.

As always, if you are serious about your personal security you need to compile a threat assessment specifically for your environment and situation and then put together some simple and practical contingency plans. The main question you need to ask yourself is do you fight or flee during a terrorist attack? The answer to this question will depend on your personal circumstances and the environmental situation.

In the United Kingdom the government guidelines for the public are to "Run, Hide, Tell", if caught up in a terrorist attack. This may fit the UK governments agenda but in real world terms it is very naive and pathetic. I understand things need to be kept simple so the general population can understand things, but... I also understand the perspective of minimalizing casualties by people not confronting armed attackers, but... I think the British bulldog attitude has long been replaced with a woke LGBTQ gerbil attitude. Where knife attacks are concerned should able bodied men run and hide and potentially leave women, young children and the elderly, who might not be able to run, to be slaughtered by some scumbag of a terrorist?

Considerations for a mass knife attack strategy

• **Pre-defined strategy:** You need to have thought about realistic responses if you are caught up in a terrorist attack. You need to do this for the areas you live and work in and locations you could be visiting. In addition to having a plan in place ensure you have the training to carry out the plan; are you physically fit enough, do you have unarmed combat or first aid training? Also, consider the fight or flee options and the ramifications of both actions.

• **Awareness:** You must always be aware of any potential security or safety threats in your environment. Without basic personal security awareness and being able to identify threats before they become incidents, your security plan is flawed.

• **Body language:** Always be observant for people who look out of place, to do this you must first of all understand the environment you are in. Always be watching for people who could be watching or following you. Always be watching for people who are acting suspiciously, who could be concealing weapons in bags or under their clothing, who are looking nervous, who are sweating too much, who are over observant etc. Learn to read peoples body language!

• **Give warning:** If you identify what you believe to be an individual or group of people acting suspiciously then report them to law enforcement or to a location's private security personnel. If you see weapons or an attack taking place raise the alarm loudly, so everyone is alerted!

• **Fight or flee:** Whether you fight or flee will depend on your responsibilities, capabilities, and your situational assessment. Are you responsible for others such as your family members who you must evacuate and protect? Are you physically capable of carrying family members or engaging in a confrontation? You must quickly assess the situation as in rapidly developing hostile incidents the time window to flee might be very small. If you choose to fight, then you must make the maximum tactical use of the environment and if you are unarmed any improvised weapons that might be available.

• **Distractions:** Always make maximum use of distractions in hostile situations. Loud noise, blinding lights, extinguishing lights to create darkness, setting off fire extinguishers, crashing shelves, smashing windows, anything to distract the attackers to give you and others time to escape or launch a counterattack.

• **Teamwork:** When counterattacking work with others to take control of the situation. A motivated and aggressive group can take the initiative away from the attackers and put them on the defensive.

• **The attack:** If you are unarmed then use whatever improvised weapons that are in your area that can be thrown or used to strike the terrorist; tables, chairs, glasses, bottles, hot coffee, scooters, cars etc. Virtually anything can be used as a weapon if you understand, how to use it, as a weapon!

• **Control:** Once the attacker is subdued or confined to a closed area you should wait for law enforcement to arrive to make the arrest etc. Remember, if you are restraining an attacker, as crazy as it might sound, you need to ensure you don't use excessive force once the attacker is under your control. Legally in most places once the attacker has surrendered and they are no longer a threat then violent force cannot be used against them. When the attacker is in your control, their safety is your responsibility.

• **Aftermath:** Once the attackers are arrested then first aid should be given to anyone who is injured. If you were involved in subduing the attackers, then take it for granted the police will be wanting to interview you for statements. Be very careful what you say to the police and if you are concerned for your legal rights then request to speak to a lawyer before giving any statements. It's a sad fact that many police force's these days do not want civilians and private security personnel confronting terrorists and criminals as they see it as their job. Their stupid perspective is if the general public starts to defend themselves from the bad guys, it brings into question why the police are not doing their job, and civilians have to defend themselves. Mature law enforcement personnel who are doing their jobs properly, understand that they need to work with the general public, but in the more woke locations where the police are pushing a political government agenda, using force to defend yourself and others from a terrorist attack can lead to you being arrested. Locations and countries where the police are hostile to civilian self-defense but are in favor of human rights for the terrorists and criminals should be avoided.

Put together a plan, get the required training, learn to read peoples body language, always be aware of security threats in your environment and you will be better prepared than most people. As

I stated at the beginning of this book most modern-day societies are seeking to demasculate their populations. If you value the safety and security of your family, your friends and yourself, you cannot become demasculated because everyone's protection is your responsibility.

VEHICLE RAMMING ATTACKS

Over the last few years there have been multiple examples of cars and trucks being used as weapons by terrorists to cause mass casualty attacks. The terrorists will always find weapons and remember they will plan their attacks to circumvent in place security hardware and protocols.

A good example of this happened on January 1st, 2025, at around 3:15 a.m. a terrorist named Shamsud-Din Jabbar, a 42-year-old American man, drove a pickup truck into a crowd on Bourbon Street in New Orleans, in the United States. He then exited the truck and engaged in a shootout with police before being fatally shot. Fourteen people were killed, plus the terrorist, and at least fifty-seven others were injured, including two police officers who were shot.

U.S. Federal law enforcement and intelligence agencies had warned local police agencies about potential vehicle-ramming attacks before the Xmas and New Year holidays. And in a 2017 memo, the New Orleans city government had also noted the risks of a mass casualty incident, including from a vehicle attack in the French Quarter, and had made plans to increase security in the area. In that same year, the New Orleans city government had bought a set of L-shaped temporary Archer vehicle barriers from Meridian Rapid Defense Group and used them to help secure the city's Mardi Gras parade against vehicle attacks. The city spent $250,000 to purchase a set of 45 Archer barriers.

On January 1st 2025 after exiting traffic, Shamsud-Din Bahar Jabbar, drove his truck onto the sidewalk to bypass a police SUV and other barricades that had been placed to protect Bourbon Street from a ramming attack. Eyewitnesses reported that steel barricades installed to prevent vehicular access were not raised before the attack, though New Orleans Police Department superintendent Anne Kirkpatrick said that police were aware they malfunctioned sometimes and instead used other barricades. The terrorist drove into people along a three-block stretch between Canal and Conti streets, at a high speed. Superintendent Kirkpatrick stated the suspect was "trying to run over as many people as he possibly could".

There are many factors that enabled this terrorist to be able to carry out his attack. The main enabler was the lax attitude of the New Orleans Police and officials who were responsible for providing security for the area. I am very sure that even though there were warnings and they had been issued barricades, their attitude was "It will never happen to us!".

Every New Years event across the United States and globally was at risk from an attack that night. I expect there were hundreds of thousands of events taking place. Out of all those events a major attack happened in New Orleans, were all those other events secure? I would expect over 90% of them were not. Why? Because it was never going to happen to them. The "It will never happen to us" attitude is a major flaw in the vast majority of security programs.

I am sure that if a member of the public, private security staff, cop or city official had raised concerns about barriers not being properly in place they would have been dismissed and laughed at for being a paranoid security geek. Those responsible for the security of most events just want to do their jobs and usually no more or less than they have to. Their aim is to get paid and go home when their shifts are over while applying minimal effort. This perspective covers the security and civil service sectors in general. Why? Because in people's minds "It will never happen to them!". Bad things only happen to other people, right?

I expect the terrorist in this attack had done his reconnaissance's at other public events prior to his attack. Maybe then he had identified that he could drive around the barriers set up to protect pedestrians on Bourbon Street. Never underestimate the bad guys as they are constantly looking and observing their potential targets for weak spots. When providing overt security for events you must ensure that visually the venue or location is a hard target and to the observer the security staff and protocols that are in place are working effectively.

Advice For The Concerned Citizen

As I have said before, do a threat assessment, put an emergency plan in place, and be aware of any security threats in your environment.

If you are attending an event where ramming could be a threat, try to assess the security for the area in advance. If you see flaws like barriers that could be driven around, then I would just avoid going to the event etc. If you try to explain a security flaw that you have seen to the event personnel or local government officials, they will 99.9% of the time just brush you off and treat you as if you are crazy. Remember, you can't educate pork, so just move on!

During an event always be aware of where there are solid natural barriers that you can get behind that would stop a speeding vehicle. If you spot a disturbance in the crowds around you do not hang around to see what's going on, move yourself and your loved ones behind hard cover as quickly as possible. And when safe to do so evacuate the area as quickly as possible using obscure routes.

Advice For The Security Provider

If you are providing the security for an event and vehicle ramming is a potential threat, then all roads and drivable routes into the event location need to be blocked and controlled. Blocked in a way that cars and trucks cannot forcefully enter the area. Vehicles that need to access the area must pass through specific control points designed to slow down and stop them while they are being checked.

This might sound simple but there can be a lot of bureaucracy, interagency cooperation, and logistics involved. To start with if roads are to be blocked who has the legal authority to block them? How will the roads be blocked? If barriers are to be used who has them? If they need to be bought who as the budget? Again, proper planning is essential to ensure that the security plan is as effective and workable as possible!

If you are working with other agencies who may be responsible for the outer cordon and control points, and you spot any flaws or gaps in their perimeter etc. you should politely report them to the event organizers and the interagency liaison. Most private security companies and police departments won't like the fact you are checking and criticizing their work but for your company's and your personal liability you need to record and report, any security issues you identify. If those who you report the issues to, choose not to act, then that's up to them.

Especially in places like the United States where you can be sued for virtually anything, you need to always cover your ass and not worry about other people's sensitivities. By recording and reporting any security issues you identify in a perimeter, or another agency's protocols you will be removing any liability that could be placed on you for security negligence in the case of a terrorist attack.

Be assured in the aftermath of a terrorist attack where there has been a failure in security procedures everyone involved will be trying to lay the blame for the security negligence on everyone else. If people have been hurt or killed due to a case of security negligence then there will be multi-million-dollar lawsuits flying in all directions, so ensure your ass is always covered!

EMERGENCY & CRISIS PLANNING

Professional emergency and crisis planning is what prevents potential problems from turning into disasters. All emergency and crisis planning needs to be kept simple and relevant to the problems they are trying to prevent or minimize. All procedures need to be rehearsed so everyone is clear on what they need to do in an emergency, talking about it is not enough. Plans discussed in comfortable meeting rooms will be enacted in a completely different manner when people are under stress, frightened and things around them are going wrong.

One thing to remember when drawing up your emergency and crisis plans is the simple truth that in reality everything will most likely go wrong. Therefore, you must try to keep your plans as simple and flexible as possible; your plans must be able to adapt to very fluid situations.

Over the years I have come across quite a few "experts" who have drawn up crisis plans for large business and government facilities that were completely unrealistic. One national organization, which had a contract with a local authority, contacted us to put together a 4-hour program designed to train unarmed county security personnel and bus drivers in anti-terrorist and hostage rescue techniques. It took numerous conversations for them to understand it takes more than 4 hours to train a SWAT team and it helps if the students have a little bit of experience. Teaching such techniques to untrained, unfit and inexperienced people simply increases the chances that if there was ever a hostage incident, they would do nothing more than escalate the situation and cause unnecessary casualties. These things are best left to the professionals.

Here are some basic considerations for putting an emergency or crisis management team and plan together for your business or facility.

Team Formation

If you need to put together a crisis team, everyone should know their responsibilities within the team and emphasis any special skills they can offer to the group.

Possible responsibilities of team members could include:

• Team commander

• Sub-commanders

• Dealing with medical emergencies

• Dealing with legal issues

• Media relations

• Security and conflict resolution

• Liaison with outside agencies

• Evacuation and lock down coordination

• Transport and vehicle marshalling

• Search and rescue

• After incident therapy

The Threat Assessment

You will need to compile a threat assessment and identify any potential threats that you or your organization may be under. You will also need to consider what assets and personnel you have available to deal with the threats. Threats could include:

• Traffic problems

- Drug use or dealing
- Work place or domestic violence
- Suicides or suicide attempts
- Indecent behavior/sexual predators
- Fire or flooding
- Natural disasters (tornados/hurricanes/earthquakes)
- Theft or loss of assets
- Intruders
- Explosive devices
- Terrorist attacks
- Kidnapping/hostage situations
- Chemical incidents

Basic things you need to consider when dealing with an incident:

- **Communications and incident reporting:** How is the alarm going to be raised and who is going to report to whom?

- **Alerting relevant parties:** How are the relevant personnel for that incident going to be alerted?

- **Incident reaction:** How are you going to deal with that incident?

There is no way I can tell you how to react to every incident, but, based upon my experience, you can expect each one to be different. I'll try to give you some guidelines to make you think, so you can develop your own strategies that are relevant to your own situations.

Here are some considerations if you are putting together emergency plans for a residence or office building. If there is a situation such as an improvised explosive device being found close to your location, you will have two basic choices: You can either stay in the building or evacuate. What you do will depend on the size and location of the device and what your building is made of.

If you choose to evacuate, you should consider:

• How will everybody be alerted to the incident?

• What are the staff responsibilities at all levels, and do those assigned responsibilities know what they are doing?

• Does everyone know the evacuation procedures for their area of the building and what exits will be used?

• Does everyone know where to go after evacuating the building?

• How will everyone be accounted for?

• Will transport be needed to get staff away from the building to a safe area?

• What first aid and emergency help will be available?

• How will people disperse after the incident?

If you choose to stay in the building, you should consider:

• How will the order for a lock down be issued to everyone?

• What are the staff responsibilities at all levels?

• Do those who are assigned responsibility know what they are doing?

• Does everyone know where the safe areas are within the building?

• How will people be alerted that the incident is over or that they need to evacuate the building?

The above is just a guide to get you thinking as emergency and crisis planning is a very detailed job. There is more to it than printing a form off of the internet and just ticking a few boxes!

ORLANDO "ANDY" WILSON

Orlando has worked internationally at all levels of the specialist security and investigation industry for over 35 years. Over the years, he has become accustomed to the types of complications that can occur, when dealing with international law enforcement agencies and the problem of dealing with kidnapping, organized crime and Mafia groups.

His experience in the international security business began in 1988 when he enlisted in the British army at 17 years of age and volunteered for a 22-month frontline, operational tour in Northern Ireland in an Infantry unit, 4 Platoon, 1 WFR. He then joined his unit's Reconnaissance Platoon, with which he undertook intensive training in small-unit warfare.

Since leaving the British army in 1993, his time spent working in Eastern Europe in the 1990s gave him firsthand experience of the operational procedures of organized criminals and Mafia groups from the former Soviet Union. In addition, he had the opportunity to oversee criminal cases that have been the first of their kind in their respective country. His operations in Mexico training tactical police teams put him in a unique position to understand the war on Narco-Terrorism. His continuous and ongoing projects focusing on kidnap and ransom prevention in South America, the Caribbean and West Africa have given him the knowledge to formulate practical programs to counter the kidnapping threat.

Orlando is a published author, writer, photographer and has been interviewed by numerous international TV and media outlets on topics ranging from kidnapping, organized crime to maritime piracy. He had his first article published in 1997 in an association magazine and his first book in 2012. He has been interviewed by media outlets ranging from the Professional Mariner Magazine,

Newsweek Serbia, Newsweek en Espanol, GrupoMilenio, Mundo-Fox, The New York Times, the BBC, Soldier of Fortune Magazine and others.

Orlando's diverse and continuous operational experience enables him to provide no-nonsense professional services and training programs. His operational investigation and close protection procedures are cutting edge and the most effective commercially available. He is also a founding member and operations manager of Risks Incorporated.

OTHER BOOKS BY ORLANDO

These Books are Available on Amazon!

Non-Fiction Manuals
• Social Navigation: A Practical Survival Guide for Human Interactions
• Counter Insurgency Operations: A tactical Guide for Law Enforcement
• Intelligence Gathering: Front Line HUMINT Considerations
• Caribbean Security Threats: A threat assessment for the islands of the Caribbean
• Gun Range Management: A Guide for Range Managers, Range Safety Officers & Firearms Instructors
• Investigative Journalist Security: Staying Alive to Tell the Truth
• Threat Assessments for Close Protection & Security Management
• Protecting Your Loved Ones: Security Awareness for Parents & Adults
• Close Protection: Luxury & Hostile Environments
• Close Protection & Firearms
• The Close Protection Business
• Home & Office Security: Protection of Residencies & Businesses
• Travel Security: Personal Travel & Vehicle Security
• Counter Terrorism: Terrorist Attack Response
• Kidnap & Ransom: The Essentials of Kidnapping Prevention
• Shoot First & Shoot Last: The Real-World Guide to Pistol Craft

Crime Fiction
• The Shoot: An Assassin's World
• Vengeance: The Art of Pain
• The Collectors: Death is Easy, Life is Hard
• Reglas Mexicanas: A Life Without Pain, Is Not A Life

Photo Books
- Athens Lockdown 2020 in Pictures
- Wandering in Serbia
- Vigilantes of Imo – Nigerian Vigilante Life in Pictures